Firing Your Boss

The Entrepreneur's Guide to Wealth Creation

Table of Contents

Chapter 1. Introduction

Unleash the entrepreneurial titan within you with our Special Report: "Firing Your Boss: The Entrepreneur's Guide to Wealth Creation". Don't let the normative cycle of a 9-to-5 job encapsulate your ambition anymore. This absolutely approachable, yet incredibly potent guide will unfurl the vital secrets of wealth creation, challenging the dominance of your disagreeable boss, and sowing the seeds for your very own venture. Brought to life by seasoned entrepreneurs and wealth creation experts, this report navigates uncharted waters in an engaging and lighthearted manner. Embrace the liberating notion of firing your boss and let us accompany you on the thrilling journey towards self-empowerment and financial independence! By the time you finish this report, not only will your mindset be invigorated with newfound resolve, but your pocket may well be lined with a boss's salary!

Chapter 2. Fanning Your Entrepreneurial Spirit

Stagnation in your career can often feel like drowning in a pool of disappointment and unfulfillment. The spark that once ignited a fiery passion has flattened into an ember, barely giving off heat. But do you know this tiny ember has the infinite potential to roar into a blazing bonfire? This ember is your entrepreneurial spirit languishing for want of proper fueling. Your task is to feed it, fan it, and let it engulf you in the warm glowing promise of prosperity and self-contentment.

'Fanning Your Entrepreneurial Spirit' does not simply mean venturing into starting a business. It is about embracing the mindset of an entrepreneur – somebody who is unafraid to take calculated risks for the prospect of high rewards, a person who thrives in the face of challenges and is adept in converting opportunities into milestones.

2.1. Identifying Your Entrepreneurial Spirit

An entrepreneur's journey begins with the identification of their entrepreneurial spirit. This spirit is characterized by resilience, adaptability, and a constant hunger for growth. It transcends the mundane and aims straight for the zenith. It questions the status quo and seeks innovation in every little act. More times than not, it will be your singular most driving force. You need to become self-aware, understand your strengths, and comprehend your motivation. Do a deep introspection. What inspires you? What makes you lose track of time? Your entrepreneurial spirit can be found in your answers to these questions.

2.2. Believing in Your Worth

As an entrepreneur, the first thing that you must sell is not your product or service, but yourself. You need to believe in your ability to make a difference. Whether it's disrupting an entire industry or simply solving a minor inconvenience for your community, you must fervently believe that you can do it! If not you, then who? This belief in your skills, coupled with a vision for change, is what attracts investments, partners, and consumers to your venture.

2.3. Harnessing Curiosity and Innovation

Interesting new ideas fuel entrepreneurship. To fan your entrepreneurial spirit, nurture a sense of curiosity that encourages you to question, experiment, and innovate. This unique combination of curiosity and innovation will allow you to see opportunities that are invisible to others. It will help you design solutions which were hitherto unimaginable. How can you make something better? How can you revamp existing systems? What new concepts can you introduce to the market? The more innovative your thinking, the bigger is your playground!

2.4. Learning from Failures

In the realm of entrepreneurship, failures are as frequent as successes. However, successful entrepreneurs know that failures are not end roads but mere detours. Each mistake made, every failure encountered, provides valuable lessons and experiences that progressively refine your entrepreneurial spirit, ultimately leading you to riches and success.

2.5. Discarding the Fear of Risks

The greatest hurdle in fanning your entrepreneurial spirit is often the looming fear of failure and risks. As an aspiring entrepreneur, you need to recognize that high risks often yield high rewards. A successful entrepreneur maintains a balanced outlook towards risks. Fear is natural, but you must not let it obstruct your actions. You need to develop risk tolerance, a quality that allows you not only to strategically evaluate risks but also to take them head-on.

2.6. Cultivating Emotional Intelligence

Entrepreneurship is not just about accurate statistics, data analysis, or impressive strategies. It is more about your emotional intelligence - understanding your emotions, empathizing with your team, and effective management of relationships. Emotional intelligence strengthens you as a person and as a leader, allowing you to perform under pressure and encouraging your entrepreneurial spirit.

2.7. Nourishing Perseverance

The world of entrepreneurship is marked by adversity. You are bound to face countless rejections, unforeseen obstacles, and possibly, devastating losses. Yet, a true entrepreneur never backs down. Perseverance keeps the embers of your entrepreneurial spirit alive. A persevering entrepreneur is like a tenacious mountain climber, undeterred by the slips and determined to reach the summit.

To sum it up, fanning your entrepreneurial spirit involves identifying and embracing your potential, fueling your curiosity and innovation, learning from failures, discarding the fear of risks, cultivating emotional intelligence, and nourishing perseverance. It is not an easy journey, but the rewards are immense. The entrepreneurial spirit within you is waiting to be unfurled, it only needs the right wind to fan it. And with these guidelines, you are now equipped to start the fire that is your entrepreneurial adventure. Let us embark on this exciting journey and witness the transformation from a tiny, smoldering ember to a roaring bonfire of prosperity and success!

Chapter 3. Dissecting the Concept of Wealth Creation

Wealth creation, so frequently discussed yet so rarely fully comprehended. The concept at first seems simple enough - increasing income or the accumulation of assets. Yet beneath this surface level understanding lies a complex web of ideas, encompassing fields as diverse as economics, psychology, sociology, and finance. Far from being a simple dollar amount in a bank account or a tally of tangible properties, true wealth represents a state of freedom, security, and opportunity.

3.1. What Exactly is Wealth Creation

Before diving deeply into the process, it's essential to clarify what wealth creation means. Despite the myriad interpretations, the principle remains the same: wealth creation is the process of deploying resources in a way that there exists a steady increase in value over time.

Wealth isn't just about money. It includes assets that could be anything from stocks, bonds, and real estate, down to intellectual property or even a robust network of contacts. It's about creating repositories of value that will grow over time. Cash sitting idly in a safety deposit box or under a mattress merely loses value to inflation while assets grow and produce more wealth, often in the form of interest, rent, dividends, or royalties.

3.2. The Financial Framework of Wealth Creation

Understanding the matrix of wealth requires a foundational grasp of the key financial principles, including the power of compound interest, the importance of diversification, and the potential for leveraging debt and risk management.

The power of compound interest, for example, is often referred to as the "eighth wonder of the world". Indeed, it is a powerful weapon that entrepreneurs can use to their advantage over extended periods. By continuously reinvesting earnings, wealth is not just incrementally but exponentially increased, demonstrating the potential for a small sum today to grow into a formidable fortune tomorrow.

Effective diversification, on the other hand, is the art of lessening your risk by spreading investments across various assets. While each individual investment carries some measure of risk - from market fluctuations, management changes, or other unforeseeable events - by diversifying the investments, investors insulate themselves from total loss.

And finally, leveraging debt and understanding risk management structure are the keys to responsible and productive use of resources to achieve more significant returns. Leveraging debt allows entrepreneurs to invest more without tying up all their personal assets. Risk management pertains to identifying, assessing, and prioritizing uncertainties and making coordinated and economical applications of resources to minimize the probable losses.

3.3. The Role of Entrepreneurship in Wealth Creation

Entrepreneurial ventures play an instrumental role in the process of wealth creation. These ventures attract capital investment because of their potential for exponential growth, thus representing significant vehicles for wealth creation. Moreover, entrepreneurship encourages innovation, driving economic development and contributing to society at large.

Entrepreneurial wealth creation is about recognizing an opportunity, innovating a solution, and enduring risks to create new products or services. These inventions and innovations add to the economy's wealth, advancing the plethora of global industries' progress, healthcare, technology, education, and many more.

3.4. The Psychological Underpinnings of Wealth

Wealth isn't just a game of numbers - it also involves the mind. It requires a psychological shift away from short-term gratification towards long-term goals. Many studies have found a correlation between an individual's mindset and their wealth-creating behavior. Individuals with an abundance mindset, for instance, are more likely to notice and capitalize on economic opportunities, whereas those with a scarcity mindset might let fear or insecurity prevent them from taking financial risks, inhibiting their wealth creation.

Creating wealth also requires resilience. The entrepreneurial journey is full of ups and downs, successes, and failures. The ability to spring back from adversity, adapt to change, and keep going in the face of failure is a common trait among effective wealth creators.

3.5. The Societal Impact of Wealth Creation

Wealth creation also has substantial societal effects. Studies show that increased wealth within a society correlates with improved levels of health, education, and well-being. As wealth is created, tax revenues increase, and can be deployed into public infrastructure, services, and social safety nets.

Wealth creation can have a cascading effect. It has the potential to reduce poverty and increase economic equality by providing jobs, stabilizing family incomes, enhancing community development, and creating wealthier societies. The prosperous populace is then able to invest in education, skills, and health, increasing productivity and promoting further economic growth.

While the concept of wealth creation may seem vast and complex, its essence is simple: consistently generating value over time. The mechanics, from the foundational aspects of financial management and entrepreneurship to the psychological and societal implications, all play essential roles in this process. By taking a long-term perspective, leveraging resources wisely, cultivating an entrepreneurial and abundance mindset, and looking to create lasting societal change, we can all become wealth creators in our own right.

Chapter 4. Saying Goodbye to Your Boss: When and How?

The critical juncture when an employee poised on the edge of entrepreneurial success chooses to cut the cord and release themselves from the comfortable binds of employment is pivotal. Saying goodbye to your boss is not just a whimsical decision, akin to changing your diet or deciding on a new hair color; it is the catapult launching you into your next phase. To simplify this complex process, we will approach it in two facets - the timing and the execution.

4.1. Timing: When is the Right Time to Say Goodbye?

Deciding when to finally hand in that resignation letter can be the source of many sleepless nights. There are however important signposts that could serve as guides on your journey.

The first indication is when you've validated your business idea. Your new venture should preferably not be a shot in the dark; rather, it should be the product of extensive research, market testing, and observations. Essentially, it's not about pulling a rabbit out of a hat but about studying the hat, the audience and their enthusiasm or lack thereof for rabbits.

Next, consider financial security. Having at least six-month worth of living expenses saved is a stark but practical approach. You might have a foolproof plan; however, going from regular paychecks to a risky venture requires you to have an adequate financial buffer.

Lastly, when your current job stands in the way of your side hustle's growth, it might be time to switch tracks. If your would-be enterprise has begun requiring a significant amount of your time and energy, it might signify that it's ready for you to take the leap.

4.2. The Execution: How to Leave Gracefully?

As romantic as the idea of burning bridges and marching out of your office blasting "I Did It My Way" through a Bluetooth speaker might seem, the real world prizes professionalism and grace.

The first step is deciding whether to disclose your plans to your boss. Depending on your relationship, it might be beneficial to tell your boss as early as possible about your decision to facilitate a smoother transition for you and your role.

Next, preparing for your exit interview. This is an opportunity for constructive feedback and a chance to leave on a good note. Offer insightful observations and professional suggestions, not an airing of personal grievances.

Moving forward, consider your resignation letter not as a goodbye note but as an official declaration of your impending departure. Maintain a professional tone and steer clear of negativity. Your letter should express gratitude for the opportunity and experience gained.

Finally, on your last days at work, make sure not to abandon your responsibilities. Tie up loose ends where you can and offer assistance in any handover processes. Leave a good last impression - remember, the business world is a tight-knit community.

Remember, there's no perfect time or foolproof way to quit your job and embark on your entrepreneurial journey, but with careful thought, financial planning and a balanced approach, you can leave the safe harbor of employment and set sail towards the thrilling journey of entrepreneurship. It's not the giant leap that most imagine but a series of small, calculated steps. Don't fear the unknown - fear staying stuck in the fortunate or unfortunate known. Aspiring entrepreneurs don't just dream; they wake up and work their dreams into reality. This means taking control, making tough decisions, and bidding your boss – and with it, your comfortable life, a respectful farewell.

Chapter 5. Blueprint for Your Own Business Venture

Building your own business venture isn't merely a process but a journey of self-discovery with each step enlightening a different aspect about you and the market you're going to delve into. Let's walk you through this blueprint for the monument of success you're about to construct.

5.1. Understanding Yourself and Your Idea

The most potent tool in your entrepreneurial journey is self-awareness. Understand your strengths, your weaknesses, and ensure that your business idea aligns with these aspects. Ask yourself what you are truly passionate about, and determine if there's a market need for it.

5.2. Laying the Market Research Foundation

Your business idea might be brilliant, but lacks viability if there's no market demand. Initiate performing a SWOT (Strengths, Weaknesses, Opportunities, Threats) analysis about your idea. Examine your potential competitors, understanding their business models, strategies, and customer bases.

5.3. Designing a Business Model

Design a business model that outlines how you create, deliver, and capture value. Consider popular models like the freemium model or subscription model, for inspiration. The crux of your model is your unique selling proposition (USP) that differentiates you from your competitors.

5.4. Building a Business Plan

A business plan isn't just for attracting investors. It serves as a roadmap for your venture. Include an executive summary, company description, market analysis, organization and management structure, product lines or services, marketing and sales strategies, and financial projections.

5.5. Testing Your Idea

Before you fully launch, validate your product or service with a minimal viable product or MVP. An MVP allows you to test your business hypothesis with real users and gain important feedback without immense financial risks.

5.6. Financing Your Venture

Consider your options: personal savings, loans, venture capital, crowdsourcing. Understand each's pros and cons and select what is right for you. Remember, initially, lean operations make sense. Cut excess and focus on necessities.

5.7. Assembling Your Team

No entrepreneur can succeed alone. Be it co-founders or first employees, ensure alignment of their vision with yours and that they complement your skill set.

5.8. Launching Your Venture

A carefully planned launch can create valuable initial momentum. Plan for a soft launch to rectify any issues before the full-fledged one.

5.9. Marketing and Sales

Find low-cost, high-impact marketing strategies that can generate sales. Consider methods like content marketing, social media marketing, influencer marketing, and SEO.

5.10. Customer Relationship Management

CRM isn't just about maintaining relationships with your customers, it's also about better understanding their needs and wants. Take criticism constructively and let it inform your product development.

5.11. Scaling Your Business

Once you've validated your model and won the first set of customers, you can focus on scaling. But remember, fast scaling could be just as harmful as no scaling if not done wisely.

5.12. Navigating the Entrepreneurial Challenges

The road to entrepreneurship is fraught with challenges. There'll be highs and lows, but it's essential to learn from failures and adapt quickly.

This foundational blueprint needs to be further refined, adjusted and actualized for your specific business venture. Remember, there are many ways to achieve entrepreneurial success, but understanding the basic anatomy of building a venture gives you the confidence and direction to conquer the business world.

Chapter 6. Risk Analysis and Management for Aspiring Entrepreneurs

Risk analysis and management constitute an integral part of the entrepreneurial journey. Whether you're planning to launch a tech start-up or an innovative clothing brand, understanding, analyzing, and mitigating risks is imperative to ensure your venture's sustainability and growth.

6.1. Understanding Risks

The first stride on this path involves understanding risks. In simple terms, a risk is any unforeseen event that could have a negative impact on your business objectives. Any business, large or small, is susceptible to risks, and as an entrepreneur, you need to identify them before they become impediments to your venture's growth and profitability. There are various kinds of risks a business may encounter – these may include operational risks, financial risks, market risks, compliance risks, and reputation risks, among others. Your first task is to identify which of these pose a threat to your specific business model.

6.2. Risk Identification

To identify potential risks, you need to thoroughly understand your business landscape. This involves a meticulous study of the industry, market, competition, and regulatory norms specific to your business sector. In risk identification, remember, the broader your scope, the better equipped your business will be to mitigate them effectively. Use tools and techniques like SWOT analysis (Strengths, Weaknesses, Opportunities, Threats), PESTEL analysis (Political, Economic, Social,

Technological, Environmental, and Legal), and Porter's Five Forces to scan the environment and identify potential risks.

6.3. Risk Assessment

Upon identification of risks, the next step entails risk assessment. This includes determining the severity of each risk, the probability of its occurrence, and the impact it may have on your venture. Risk severity, or magnitude, is measured in terms of financial loss, operational inefficiencies, or reputational damage that a risk event could cause. Risk occurrence probability gauges how likely it is for the risk to materialize. Finally, risk impact assessment tries to quantify the actual damage, in measurable terms, like financial loss, that the risk can cause. Use tools like Risk Impact/Probability Chart to prioritize risks based on these parameters.

6.4. Risk Response

After the risks have been assessed, the next step is to determine the best response strategy. There are four main risk response strategies you can employ:

1. Mitigation: Here, steps are taken to reduce the impact or likelihood of the risk. For instance, training staff to manage technology-related risks.

2. Acceptance: This strategy involves accepting the risk without taking any action. This is usually followed when the cost of countering the risk outweighs the benefits.

3. Transfer: Risks can be transferred to a third party through insurance, outsourcing, or agreements.

4. Avoidance: This involves changing your business strategy to completely avoid the risk. It's typically used for risks with high potential for damage.

The choice of strategy depends on your assessment of the risk's severity, probability, and potential impact.

6.5. Risk Monitoring and Review

Remember, risk management is a continuous process. After your risk responses have been implemented, it's critical to monitor and review the situation. This helps in understanding how effectively risks are being managed and whether any adjustments are required. It's essential to keep your risk management strategies flexible and make adjustments as new risks emerge.

As part of the review process, entrepreneurs can use Key Risk Indicators (KRIs) – metrics that help in understanding the impact of risks and the effectiveness of the strategies employed.

6.6. Creating a Risk Management Plan

A risk management plan documents your approach to managing risks. It consists of the identified risks, their assessments, chosen response strategies, and monitoring methods. It's an integral part of your overall business plan and serves as a crucial blueprint when dealing with uncertainties in your venture.

Evidently, risk analysis and management are not just about avoiding losses or preventing negative occurrences but are also about understanding vulnerabilities and transforming them into opportunities. As an aspiring entrepreneur, taking the calculated leap after considering potential risks and planning the right mitigations will prove vital in carving your own entrepreneurial path. With a well-thought-out risk management plan, you'll be better prepared for unexpected hurdles and will be in a stronger position to lead your venture to success.

Chapter 7. Fundamentals of Financial Independence

To jumpstart this whirlwind voyage of wealth creation and entrepreneurial triumph, it's paramount that we begin by laying the cornerstone upon which your financial sovereignty will be built.

Understanding the fundamentals of financial independence flows not only from grasping the mechanisms of income generation but also unravelling the mysteries of wealth protection, smart investing, debt management, tax efficiency, retirement planning, and more. Let's deftly delve into these waters, one drop at a time:

7.1. Understanding your Current Financial Status

To skilfully navigate the path to financial independence, the first stop is your current financial status. Understand your income streams, monthly expenditure, savings ratio, outstanding debts, and net worth. Keep track of these parameters to enable you to effectively sculpt your plan of action. A meticulous review of these factors can be illuminating, setting a clear starting point for your financial journey.

List down your assets and liabilities to calculate your net worth. Assets comprise cash, savings, real estate, stock investments, and personal items of considerable worth. Liabilities are your financial obligations, including mortgages, loans, and credit card debts. Net worth provides an instant financial snapshot, helping to establish your baseline and track progress.

7.2. Building an Emergency Fund

Before diving into the world of entrepreneurship, it's wise to secure an emergency fund. An unforeseen event should not derail your journey to financial independence. The fund should ideally cover 6 to 12 months' worth of living expenses, but this range can be adjusted as per your personal comfort and risk tolerance.

The fund acts as a financial floatation device, providing you the peace of mind to navigate the obstacles and uncertainties that your entrepreneurial journey may bring.

7.3. Understanding the Power of Compounding

Albert Einstein called the power of compounding the 'eighth wonder of the world'. Compounding allows for exponential growth of your savings and investments. A consistent investment, no matter how small, in a growth-oriented instrument will accumulate and multiply over a period, with interest growing on the initial investment as well as the previously accrued interest.

It's a critical funda that paves the way for accelerated wealth creation. Initiate your investment journey as early as possible to optimally leverage this powerful tool.

7.4. Debt Management

Educate yourself about good debt versus bad debt. A mortgage loan for a home or a business loan for expanding operations can be seen as good debt because they are forms of investing in appreciating assets. In contrast, credit card debts from unnecessary splurges fall into the realm of bad debt.

Effective debt management involves paying off high-interest debts first, maintaining a good credit score, and balancing 'good' debt with other investment avenues. It's also crucial to have a regular review mechanism, ensuring you never fall into a debt trap.

7.5. Income Diversification

Possessing a single income stream is a risk best avoided in our tumultuous economic landscape. It's prudent to diversify, deriving income from varied sources like rental properties, secure bonds, mutual funds, stocks, or a side business. Diversification serves as a safety net, cushioning the impact of market fluctuations.

7.6. Savvy Tax Planning

Efficient tax planning ensures that you retain maximum income by exploiting legal exemptions, deductions, and benefits. Consult a tax advisor or take the time to understand tax-saving investments and schemes available in your country. With smart planning, taxes should become hurdles you can skillfully dodge on your way to financial independence.

7.7. Retirement Planning

Retirement planning directly ties in with financial independence. Forecasting future cash flow requirements, understanding the time value of money, and regular investing in retirement funds are aspects of securing a financially stable retirement. Be proactive in understanding various retirement plans and schemes and plan accordingly.

This multitude of aspects collectively forms the bedrock of financial independence. The grasp of these fundamentals will enable you to wield your finances as an instrument of liberty, allowing you to confidently 'fire' your boss and stride toward the terrain of entrepreneurship. On this journey, remember that financial independence is not achieved overnight. It's a process of building and securing a financial fortress step by careful step. A disciplined and patient approach will lead you to the ultimate aim of this journey: a life unshackled from financial constraints, carving out your entrepreneurial destiny.

Chapter 8. Your Business, Your Brand: Understanding Market Positioning

As an entrepreneur, your brand is your promise to your customers. It tells them what they can expect from your products and services, and how you differ from your competition. Your brand is derived from who you are, who you want to be, and how people perceive you to be.

8.1. Building Brand Identity

The elements that encapsulate your brand include your logo, website, packaging, promotional materials, all of which should integrate your logo and messaging. They should consistently communicate your brand. Your brand strategy is how, what, where, when and to whom you communicate your brand messages.

On the other hand, the foundation of your brand is your logo. Your website, packaging and promotional materials should integrate your logo and extend your brand strategy.

While a professional logo and website are important investments, the real work begins with the development of your brand's true essence, the creation of a unique, compelling and distinct brand identity.

8.2. Understanding Your Audience

Before you start the process of brand positioning, it's important to understand your target audience. These are the people who are most likely to buy from you. They could be existing customers, potential customers, and people who have shown interest in your product or service.

To understand your audience, answer the following questions: - What problems does your product or service solve for them? - Why do they choose your products or services instead of your competitors? - What do they value most about what you offer?

Understanding your audience is crucial to defining your brand and positioning yourself in the marketplace.

8.3. Competitive Analysis

The next step in your understanding of market positioning is competitive analysis. You have to know your competition to set yourself apart from them. Look at their branding and marketing strategies, their offerings, and their pricing.

You need to identify what makes you different and better. This will become your unique selling proposition (USP) - the main reason why customers should choose your products or services over those of your competitors.

8.4. Unique Selling Proposition (USP)

The Unique Selling Proposition (USP) is what separates your business from the competition. It highlights the unique benefit or advantage that only your business can offer to customers.

A clearly defined USP helps customers understand why they should choose your business over others. The USP should be integrated into all your brand's marketing and promotional activities.

8.5. Brand Story

The heart of your brand is a story. This story should encapsulate what your brand stands for, it's history, and what it's aiming to achieve. This often helps to build an emotional connection with customers, helping to align your values with theirs.

8.6. Brand Promise

Your brand promise is what customers can expect when they interact with your brand. It's about the experience that you vow to give them - how you promise to make them feel. This is a critical part of defining your brand and should be reflected throughout all of your messaging.

8.7. Positioning Statement

Your brand positioning statement is a brief statement that clearly articulates your brand's unique value proposition compared to your competitors. It should effectively communicate the benefits of your products or services and what makes it different and better.

8.8. Brand Touchpoints

Brand touchpoints are any points of contact between your brand and your customers. Brand touchpoints are opportunities to position your company, to enhance customer experience, and to create memorable, positive associations with your brand.

8.9. Consistency in Brand Messaging

Consistency promises to deliver the same experience every time your customers come into contact with your brand. Consistency sets up expectations for your brand that you must fulfill.

Once you've defined your brand and understood your positioning, the next step is creating a strategy to effectively communicate that positioning to your target market. The goal is to create a strong, consistent image and message that resonates with your customers.

In the end, remember - your business, your brand. This is not a one-and-done type of scenario. Brand building is a continuous process that requires time, effort, and consistency. So keep reinforcing your brand and positioning, because that's what will make you stand out in the marketplace.

Chapter 9. Leadership Transformation: From Employee to Employer

Consider your transition from employee to employer an evolution, an immense metamorphosis akin to a caterpillar transforming into a butterfly. Your journey won't be swift or seamless. Rather, it will consist of various stages, requiring determination, patience, and a radical mindset shift.

9.1. Embracing an Entrepreneurial Mindset

An essential prerequisite to this transformation is adopting an entrepreneur's mindset. It involves the willingness to take risks, the thirst for continuous learning, the capacity to face failure, and a relentless commitment to realizing your visions.

Risks are an inevitable part of the journey. Embrace them, learn from them. More often than not, the fear of being wrong, making mistakes, or failure can be paralyzing. Shunning this fear is the fundamental step towards taking risks. Remember, every successful entrepreneur has had their fair share of failure. It is through making mistakes that learning and future innovation occur.

The entrepreneurial journey involves continuous learning and adaptation. Being able to understand industry trends, technological advancements, customer expectations, and market dynamics, and applying these learnings to your business, will differentiate you from others. Maintaining intellectual curiosity and always staying receptive to new ideas are the bedrock of constant learning.

As an entrepreneur, your vision is your compass. It is the one constant in the ever-changing landscape of business. Jean Elie, a successful entrepreneur, once said, "The vision must be followed by the venture. It is not enough to stare up the steps - we must step up the stairs." This quote beautifully encapsulates how an entrepreneur's vision is what motivates, drives, and enables them to overcome obstacles and navigate success.

9.2. The Skill of Decision Making

Decision making is an essential skill to foster as a business owner. As an employee, the weight of most business decisions doesn't fall directly upon your shoulders. In contrast, as an entrepreneur, every decision you make, from the trivial to the pivotal, has the potential to hugely impact your business. Your decisions can dictate every aspect from strategy formulation to everyday operations.

To hone your decision-making abilities, adopt a fact-driven approach. Since the business environment is a complex and dynamic system, making an informed decision requires a careful analysis of data and information. You might need to engage in an iterative process of hypothesis formation, data collection, analysis, and reflection to arrive at the best outcome.

Critical thinking, too, is invaluable in the decision-making process. Challenge existing norms and beliefs, assess situations from multiple perspectives, and look for non-conventional solutions. Constantly question if there is a better or innovative way to perform a task or solve a problem.

Recognize that a great deal of decision making involves risk-taking. Making the perfect decision isn't always possible. More often than not, you'll need to take calculated risks. And, even in unsuccessful attempts, there can be significant learning and growth.

9.3. Cultivating Leadership Skills

As the keystone of your business venture, your leadership style will crucially determine the culture, values, and productivity of your organization. One of the most common pitfalls for new entrepreneurs is to take on too much by themselves. Delegation is a critical leadership skill because it empowers your team, frees up your time for strategic planning, and builds a culture of trust.

Another leadership skill to hone is communication. Be transparent and open, clearly articulate your expectations, listen actively, and be flexible in handling responses. Good communication nurtures a productive environment and strengthens relationships within your team.

Effective leaders embody empathy. Understanding the needs, concerns, and ambitions of your team allows you to guide and support them effectively. Empathy fosters a work atmosphere where individuals feel valued and cared for, leading to high morale and productivity.

9.4. Journey from a Secure Paycheck to Uncertain Profits

Last but certainly not least, is overcoming the fear of losing your steady paycheck. The risky nature of entrepreneurship and the possibility of inconsistent revenue can be daunting. It is essential to strategize and plan for your financial management as you transition from a fixed income to a variable profit.

A reserve fund is the first thing you should consider. This is a safety net that helps you manage your living costs during your start-up phase and can also serve as a backup for unexpected business expenses.

As part of your financial planning, you also need to be very clear about your business costs. Understand the dynamics of fixed costs, variable costs, and potential hidden expenditures, to avoid any troublesome financial surprises later.

Also, remember that while the financial stakes are undoubtedly high, so are the potential rewards. As an entrepreneur, your earnings aren't limited to a fixed salary but instead directly connected to your business's success.

All these aspects represent the multi-dimensional transformation you will undergo from an employee to an entrepreneur. The journey may be challenging, and at times, overwhelming, but ultimately your determination, courage, and entrepreneurial spirit will lead you to extraordinary wealth creation and self-empowerment.

Chapter 10. Sustaining Your Business: Beginner to Beyond

Success is not a one-time achievement but an ongoing process that requires continuous effort and vigilance. Creating a business from scratch is a commendable achievement in itself, but the real challenge lies in maintaining that success and ensuring your enterprise's longevity. This chapter will provide you with comprehensive guidance on how to sustain your business, nurturing its growth from its nascent state and beyond.

10.1. Understanding Your Market

One of the fundamental aspects of running a successful business is understanding your market. It's important to know what your customers want and how their needs may change over time. You ought to keep abreast of changes in your industry and adapt your business strategies accordingly. It involves researching your competitors, understanding market trends, customer preferences, and global economic changes.

Conduct regular market analysis to comprehend your niche deeply. Stay open to fresh ideas and trends that can enhance your offering. Understanding your market helps keep your service or product relevant, boosts your competitiveness, and creates opportunities for expansion.

10.2. Building Robust Financial Management

Financial management is key to the survival and growth of any business. A deep understanding of your cost structures, cash flow, and profitability is crucial for identifying opportunities and risks alike. Implement a budget, and adhere to it. Always keep some cash reserve for emergencies and unexpected costs.

Engage with a financial advisor or take courses in financial management to ensure your knowledge is up to date. Use modern financial tools and software to streamline your business operations. Proper financial management not only helps in maintaining your business but also enables future growth.

10.3. Fostering Strong Customer Relationships

Your customers are your business's lifeblood. Without them, your business is unlikely to survive. Building and nurturing strong relationships with your customers should be a priority. Earning customer loyalty can be more valuable than acquiring new customers.

Take the time to communicate with your customers, understand their needs, and provide excellent service. Regularly receive feedback and act upon it. Personalize your interactions to make each customer feel valued. Loyal customers not only bring repeat business, but they also become brand advocates, providing free advertising and positive reviews.

10.4. Developing Your Team

You might start your business as a solo entrepreneur, but as your business expands, you'll likely need a dedicated team. Choosing the right people to join your team can make or break your business. Invest in training and development to enhance your team's skills and capabilities.

Building a culture that encourages creativity, innovation, and collaboration can increase productivity and job satisfaction. Promote open communication and regularly provide constructive feedback to create a supportive work environment. A motivated and capable team stands as a robust pillar for business sustainability.

10.5. Continuous Innovation and Adaptability

With an ever-changing business landscape, adaptability and innovation are paramount to staying relevant and competitive. Regularly review and update your products and services to meet changing customer needs. Keep abreast with technological advancements to streamline operations and enhance productivity.

Disruptive innovations can threaten your business, but they can also provide opportunities for growth. Stay vigilant and be prepared to pivot when necessary. Remember, being stubbornly tied to your original business plan without considering changes in the market landscape can lead to your business's downfall.

10.6. Building Strategic Partnerships

Strategic partnerships can offer significant benefits to your business, from opening up new markets, sharing resources, to enhancing credibility. Align with other businesses that complement yours and can bring mutual benefits. Such partnerships can stimulate business growth and promote sustainability.

Despite the numerous advantages, remember to approach each partnership with caution. Thoroughly investigate potential partners and negotiate agreements that protect your business interests and maintain your company's independence and freedom.

10.7. Emphasis on Sustainable Practices

Sustainability goes beyond just maintaining your business. It also involves making your business environmentally sustainable by adopting greener practices. These can range from reducing waste, using sustainable materials, to promoting energy efficiency.

A sustainable business not only makes a positive impact on the environment, but it can also enhance your brand image and appeal to a segment of conscious consumers. Including sustainability as part of your business strategy also prepares your business to meet any future regulatory requirements that promote environmental conservation.

In conclusion, sustaining your business is a complex task that requires continuous effort, adaptability, and savvy business skills. By successfully implementing these strategies, you can build a resilient business capable of withstanding challenges and navigating the turbulent waters of the business world. Remember that entrepreneurship is a journey, not a destination, so stay focused, stay learning, and always aim for growth.

Chapter 11. Planning for Prosperity: Future-Proofing Your Wealth

An entrepreneurial endeavour is more than just bidding adieu to the customary 9-to-5 job; it's about building a secure financial future. What lies ahead is a comprehensive rundown of steps that must be endorsed on your journey to a prosperous business.

11.1. Building a Financial Foundation

Let's begin by laying a strong financial foundation. This is similar to building a house; without a stable foundation, it will eventually collapse.

Start Saving Now: Ignite the engine of your venture by gradually saving a portion from your existing income. Trying to save something between 20-30% of your income can make a significant difference.

Emergency Funds: Always be prepared for unpredicted hindrances. An emergency fund acts as a safety net in such circumstances, preventing your venture from debilitation during financial downturns.

Clear Your Debts: Debt is the biggest constraint in creating wealth. Start by paying off your high-interest debts then move on to others.

11.2. Investing Your Money

Once you have a stable base, proceed ahead by learning how to grow that money, which involves strategic investments. Here's how you can steadily increase your wealth:

Understand Different Investment Options: Diversify your investment portfolio to draw profit from different sectors. It can include stocks, real estate, mutual funds and even cryptocurrency depending on your risk tolerance.

Learn About Compound Interest: Compound interest is one of the most powerful tools for wealth creation. Recognize how it can grow your wealth exponentially over time.

Invest Regularly: A consistent investment routine will ensure that your wealth grows steadily, outpacing inflation and yielding considerable returns over time.

11.3. Designing a Business Plan

Every triumphant entrepreneur is backed by a sound business plan. Your business plan acts as a roadmap leading you towards your goal.

Analyze Your Market: Understand your target audience, their needs, and how you can fulfill these needs with your product or service.

Set S.M.A.R.T. Goals: Set specific, measurable, achievable, relevant and time-bound goals for your business. These goals provide a clear milestone and direction to assist your progression.

Plan Finances: Outline the financial aspect including start-up costs, projected profits, and break-even point.

11.4. Tax Planning

Taxation forms a significant part of your financial planning. Understanding how to navigate through it can help you save more of what you earn.

Understand Tax Laws: Comprehend the existing tax laws in your country and identify how you can use them to your advantage.

Utilize Tax Deductions: Various expenditures related to your business can be tax-deductible. These deductions can significantly reduce your taxable income.

Hire a Tax Consultant: Tax planning becomes increasingly complex as your wealth grows. Consider hiring a tax consultant who can guide you through the process and help save money.

11.5. Risk Management

Stepping into an entrepreneurial venture involves dealing with various types of risks. Knowing how to manage these risks will ensure your venture's survival.

Identify Risks: Figure out potential risks that can affect your business; it could be operational, financial or market-related.

Formulate a Contingency Plan: Having a backup plan helps to combat unforeseen events threatening your venture and possibly, your wealth.

Insure Your Business and Assets: Protect your venture and personal assets from any potential damage or lawsuits through proper insurance.

Remember, the journey to prosperity is not a sprint; it's a marathon. It requires diligent planning, sensible decision-making, and enduring perseverance. Equipped with these attributes and this simple guide to future-proofing your wealth, you stand a good chance at flourishing as a financially successful entrepreneur.

www.ingramcontent.com/pod-product-compliance
Lightning Source LLC
Chambersburg PA
CBHW071044260726
48661CB00007B/3145